REDEEMED

from

DEATH

Receiving God's Promise of
Long Life in the Earth & Eternity

T0015164

Bill Winston

Published by HigherLife Publishing & Marketing, Inc.
PO Box 623307
Oviedo, FL 32762
AHigherLife.com

Cover and Interior Design by Faithe Thomas, Master Design Marketing, LLC

ISBN (Paperback): 978-1-958211-06-9

ISBN (Ebook): 978-1-958211-07-6

Library of Congress # 1-11037284980

Printed in the United States of America.

10 11 12 13 — 9 8 7 6 5 4 3 2 1

Contents

Contents

Introduction

THERE IS NO MORE important subject in the Christian faith than the reality of redemption, which I am teaching in this book. Redemption goes beyond your eternal salvation; it covers every area of life here on earth before you get to heaven.

In *Redeemed from Death: Receiving God's Promise of Long Life in the Earth and Eternity*, we will examine God's promise in the Bible for you to have a long, satisfying life that will be a blessing—not only to you but also to your family, community, and beyond.

Let's start with the definition of *redeemed*, which means "to be brought back or bought back." We were in captivity, but we've been brought out of that captivity. What we want to do now is understand what it means to be brought out of death into life.

As we dive into what the Word of God says about our redemption, we will see that we can put death on the shelf until we have lived full lives and are ready for it. It's not up to death to dictate when or how we should pass from this life. Putting death in the warehouse, so to speak, until we are ready for it allows us to lead a life free from the fear of death.

Our objective is to take away all fear of death because we were never meant to have fear. Sometimes death seems to stalk people. Some people consider it morbid to even talk about it. You see, people show up at funerals that you haven't seen in years and even decades, and just the word *death* sends chills of fear and sorrow through them.

This shouldn't be! The apostle Paul said, "Beloved brothers and sisters, we want you to be quite certain about the truth concerning those who have passed away, so that you won't be overwhelmed with grief like many others who have no hope" (1 Thessalonians 4:13 TPT).

In *Redeemed from Death: Receiving God's Promise of Long Life in the Earth and Eternity*, you will learn how:

- All humanity is facing a death sentence.
- Death is an enemy of God and didn't come from Him.
- Fear robs you of enjoying life and fulfilling your earthly assignment.

- It is not God's will for you to die after seventy or eighty years.
- Through Jesus Christ, God's mandate to have dominion over the earth has been restored.

God created you and placed you in the earth *for such a time as this*. He has given you a divine assignment that can only be accomplished through faith. As you learn to dominate and take control over fear and death, you will be able to enjoy life fully—and joyfully fulfill your God-given destiny!

CHAPTER 1

Mysteries Unraveled

Howbeit we speak wisdom among them that are perfect: yet not the wisdom of this world, nor of the princes of this world, that come to nought: but *we speak the wisdom of God in a mystery, even the hidden wisdom,* **which God ordained before the world unto our glory: which none of the princes of this world knew: for had they known it, they would not have crucified the Lord of glory.**
—1 Corinthians 2:6–8 emphasis added

GOD'S PLAN WAS A mystery! The devil didn't know what Jesus was doing because satan, who was once Lucifer and covered the throne of God, had lost his anointing for wisdom. The rulers of this world were blinded and didn't understand that Jesus is the

Messiah called by God to save them. How did this all come about?

The Origin of Death

Let's look, first of all, back to the origin of death. Go with me to Genesis 1:26: "And God said, Let us make man in our image, after our likeness: and let them have dominion over the fish of the sea, and over the fowl of the air, and over the cattle, and over all the earth, and over every creeping thing that creepeth upon the earth."

This is talking about the creation of man. God created man out of literally *nothing*. He made man out of that which you couldn't see. This part of man that He's talking about is the real man. In other words, God created man out of that which is spirit. He created man in His own image and after His likeness, meaning that image is the exact duplicate in kind. If I look in a mirror, what do I see? My image. If you look at a man whom God created, you're going to see what God looks like.

Let Them Have Dominion

Now, I'm not trying to bring God down to some natural level, but I'm saying this: when Adam was first created, he was created to be the exact duplicate of God. God made Adam, and then God said, "Let them have dominion." He didn't say, "Let *Us* have dominion"; He said, "Let *them* have dominion."

The Bible describes the next stage of how God made man: "And the LORD God formed man of the dust of the ground, and breathed into his nostrils the breath of life; and man became a living soul" (Genesis 2:7).

Note that this time it says that God *formed* man of the dust of the ground. This word *formed* is a different Hebrew word than the one used for *created*. *Formed* means "to mold from a substance that already exists." God used the elements of the soil to form man's body. Then He breathed into Adam's nostrils and man became a living soul.

Spirit, Soul, and Body

Adam was made up of three parts: spirit, soul, and body. His body made contact with the outer material world. It was linked to his spirit through his soul. His soul was his mind, will, emotions, intellect, and imagination. These parts function together, but the real man is the invisible spirit inside—the exact image and duplicate of God.

What happened next? God put man in the garden that He had prepared for mankind.

> **And the LORD God took the man, and put him into the garden of Eden to dress it and to keep it. And the LORD God commanded the man, saying, Of every tree of the garden thou mayest freely eat: but of the tree of the knowledge of good and evil, thou shalt not eat of it: for in the day that thou eatest thereof thou shalt surely die.**
>
> —Genesis 2:15–17

You've Got Potential!

Here God placed a demand on man's potential. The first thing He did was give Adam work. God has divine purpose behind our working; it is beyond just a paycheck. One of the reasons for work is that there is potential inside you. As you work, you develop that potential to better serve those around you. In other words, you don't go to work for a living; you go to work for a giving.

You've got potential, but there's a condition. God gave Adam (and Eve) a prohibition. He told them, "Don't eat of that tree, I command you, for the day you eat of that tree you shall surely die." He didn't say it was a fifty-fifty chance either. No, He said, "If you eat of that one tree, you've got a 100-percent chance that you're going to die."

Notice what God was doing. He was exercising man's free will to choose to obey or not to obey. God exercised Adam's intellect by having him name the animals. God was exercising the imagination. In the same way God brought out Adam's potential, He will develop the potential inside of you.

Their Eyes Were Opened

When God told Adam he would surely die if he ate of the forbidden tree, He was not talking *to* his flesh, and He was not talking *about* his flesh. He was talking about *his spirit*—the real him. Adam (and Eve) had been warned. You know the story: Eve ate of the fruit and gave it to Adam, who also ate.

Let's pick the story back up in Genesis 3: "And the eyes of them both were opened, and they knew that they were naked; and they sewed fig leaves together, and made themselves aprons" (Genesis 3:7).

After they disobeyed God's command and realized they were naked, their spiritual eyes were now shut. Why? Because their spirits went dead to God. Two things happened here: One, they were separated from God; and two, they took on the nature of the devil— the nature of iniquity and death. They took on death.

Adam and Eve, and as a result all mankind, could no longer see spiritually, so part of their vision was cut off. They could only function from the realm of their senses and their souls rather than from the realm of their spirits. The spectrum of their reality had been closed.

The Blame Game

Adam was in the garden and heard God calling him, asking where he was, so Adam replied, "I was afraid because I was naked, so I went and hid myself." He was hiding from the very One that created him.

God asked more questions: "Who told you that you were naked? Have you eaten of the tree I told you not to eat?"

Adam put the blame on God: "The woman You gave me, she gave it to me and I ate."

Then Eve defended herself and shifted the blame too, saying: "The serpent (satan) tempted me and I ate."

God pronounced a curse on satan. He pronounced judgment on him, saying, "The seed of a woman is going to bruise your head." (See Genesis 3:10–15.)

Another Mystery Unfolds

The woman whose Seed did this was, of course, Mary. Let's jump from Genesis for a moment to a mystery that would be made manifest thousands of years later. Satan understood there would be One who would fulfill God's judgment: "Jesus made a public spectacle of all the powers and principalities of darkness, stripping away from them every weapon and all their spiritual authority and power" (Colossians 2:15 TPT).

What the enemy (satan) didn't understand was the prophesied virgin birth. God sent an angel to a woman named Mary. The angel told Mary she was going to have a child who would be the Son of God.

Mary questioned how this was going to happen to her, a virgin, and the angel went on to say that the Holy Spirit would come upon her. Mary agreed, saying, "Be it unto me according to thy word" (Luke 1:38), and she supernaturally received the Seed.

It's a Holy Seed

Where did this Seed come from? God. It didn't come from a natural man because Mary knew no man. Understand, she got the Seed from God. Mary supplied the body; God supplied the life. She supplied the wrapping. This earth suit is my wrapping.

If satan had understood God's prophetic plan to save mankind through this Seed, he wouldn't have crucified Jesus. Why? Because through the crucifixion and resurrection of Jesus, satan actually *planted* Him.

Get it? What do you do with a seed? You plant it! If the devil had known that his crucifying Jesus was going to plant Him in the earth and that in three days He was going to come back up and all of us would be saved, he never would have done it!

Ye Are (Little *G*) Gods

Let's go back to Genesis again. Satan thought he had the victory when he tempted Eve in the garden because God had given Adam a prohibition: "Of every tree of the garden thou mayest freely eat: but of the tree of the knowledge of good and evil, thou shalt not eat of it: for in the day that thou eatest thereof thou shalt surely die" (Genesis 2:16–17).

"And the serpent said unto the woman, Ye shall not surely die: for God doth know that in the day ye eat thereof, then your eyes shall be opened, and ye shall be as gods, knowing good and evil" (Genesis 3:4–5).

What Eve didn't realize was that they were already as gods (little *g*). Psalm 82:6 says, "I have said, Ye are gods; and all of you are children of the most High." The enemy deceived Eve into seeking something she already possessed! We see this reflected in an earlier scripture: "God said, Let us make man in *our image*, after *our likeness*: and let them have *dominion*" (Genesis 1:26 emphasis added).

God is the big G God, and we are the little *g* gods made in His image and likeness. God gave us dominion over all the earth. Through sin and disobedience,

Adam lost this dominion and turned it over to satan, who became the god of this world. (See 2 Corinthians 4:4.) But that's not the end of the story—there's good news, as we'll discover in later chapters of this book.

CHAPTER 2

Death Sentence

IN THE LAST CHAPTER, we talked about the Seed of a woman. The first seed was in Adam, but that seed in Adam was now contaminated, so God had to get another Seed back into the earth.

Who is this perfect Seed that was not contaminated like man's seed? Scripture says, "The first man, Adam, became a living soul. The last Adam became the life-giving Spirit" (1 Corinthians 15:45 TPT). This same verse in the *Contemporary English Version* says it plainly: "The first man was named Adam, and the scriptures tell us that he was a living person. But Jesus, who may be called the last Adam, is a life-giving spirit."

Notice what Jesus is called. He is called "a life-giving spirit," or as it says in the King James Version, "the last Adam was made a quickening spirit."

Jesus Came to Destroy the Works of the Devil

Jesus was sent by the Father to the earth for a purpose: "For this purpose the Son of God was revealed, that He might destroy the works of the devil" (1 John 3:8 MEV). What are the works of the devil? Satan wants to separate man from God for eternity, which is spiritual death.

We read earlier about how Adam was cut off because he violated the command God gave him not to eat of the tree in the midst of the garden. What we want to know is what happened to Adam. What made him slip? In the beginning, he wasn't perfect, but he was innocent.

God gave Adam a free will just as He gave a free will to you and me and all mankind. Adam used his free will to sin, which caused him to be cut off from God. This is spiritual death. And just like God said he would, Adam died—spiritually!

When a person dies spiritually, they're immediately separated from God. When they are separated from God, that separation (or death) is instant. The moment

Adam violated God's command, Adam died. He became spiritually dead.

Man Was Made to Live Forever

Adam's body took another nine hundred years or so to die because he really didn't know how to die. He wasn't made to die. He was made to live forever, but he died. Even though he died instantly in the spirit, Adam's physical death was progressive. It took time.

Death doesn't come from God; it comes from the one who perverted things, and that's the devil. God is not the author of death. He is not taking you out of here with death. Anybody that God took, He took alive!

Like Enoch:

> **So Enoch lived a total of 365 years.**
> **Enoch walked with God [he had a close**
> **relationship with God]; one day Enoch**
> **could not be found, because God took**
> **him [like Elijah, he did not die].**
>
> —Genesis 5:23–24 EXB

Like Elijah:

> **As they were walking along and talking, a**
> **chariot of fire and horses of fire appeared**

and separated [drove between] Elijah from
Elisha. Then Elijah went up [ascended] to
heaven in a whirlwind.

—2 Kings 2:11 EXB

And of course, like Jesus:

These were his last words. As they watched,
he was taken up and disappeared in a cloud.
They stood there, staring into the empty
sky. Suddenly two men appeared—in white
robes! They said, "You Galileans!—why
do you just stand here looking up at an
empty sky? This very Jesus who was taken
up from among you to heaven will come as
certainly—and mysteriously—as he left."

—Acts 1:9–11 MSG

A Dead Man Walking

Here was Adam, a dead man (spiritually), walking
around. It was just a matter of time before his physical
body also ceased to exist. Adam's spirit not only died
to God, but it was changed and took on a new nature.
He took on the nature of the one he followed—satan.
Adam took on a satanic nature called *iniquity* or *death*.

Where Adam had life in him before, he was now filled with death.

Now Adam and God were not talking anymore. Think about it this way: I'm talking on the telephone and somebody kicks the plug or pulls the phone out of the wall or loses their internet connection. I'm saying, "Hello? Hello? Hello?" The person on the other side is also saying, "Hello? Hello? Hello?" But we can't hear each other because we are now *disconnected*. That is what happened when death came into the human race.

God says, "Adam, the day that you eat of this, you shall surely die. The sentence for this transgression, Adam, is eternal death. That's what you're going to get. If you eat of this, your sentence is eternal death."

Jesus Served the Death Sentence in Your Place

Jesus came to the earth to be the substitute for man. He was the sacrifice to pay for man's sin. He took man's place. Now, a physical death alone wouldn't have done any good, because if it had been enough, Abel's death and his blood would've taken care of it. But it didn't. Human blood wasn't sufficient because of sin. This sacrifice had to be spotless blood. Only Jesus had spotless blood.

On the cross alongside Him, the thief said to Jesus,

> **"Jesus, [please] remember me when You come into Your kingdom!" Jesus said to him, "I assure you *and* most solemnly say to you, today you will be with Me in Paradise."**
>
> **...And Jesus, crying out with a loud voice, said, "Father, INTO YOUR HANDS I COMMIT MY SPIRIT!" Having said this, He breathed His last.**
>
> —Luke 23:42–43, 46 AMP

Verse 46 in the King James Version says it this way: "And when Jesus had cried with a loud voice, he said, Father, into thy hands I commend my spirit: and having said thus, he gave up the ghost."

Jesus Died Two Deaths

Jesus gave up the ghost—He was separated from God. How could Jesus die? He could only die physically because He died spiritually first. If He hadn't died spiritually, they couldn't have killed Him. He had to die spiritually before the physical death of his body could occur.

> He was taken from prison and from
> judgment:
> and who shall declare his generation?
> for he was cut off out of the land of the
> living:
> for the transgression of my people was he
> stricken.
> And he made his grave with the wicked,
> and with the rich in his *death*;
> because he had done no violence,
> neither was any deceit in his mouth.
>
> —Isaiah 53:8–9 emphasis added

See that word *death*? In Hebrew, it's plural. He died two ways: spiritually and naturally (or physically). Because Jesus died two ways, both physically and spiritually, He went to hell when He died.

> Ye men of Israel, hear these words; Jesus of
> Nazareth, a man approved of God among
> you by miracles and wonders and signs,
> which God did by him in the midst of you,
> as ye yourselves also know: him, being
> delivered by the determinate counsel and

foreknowledge of God, ye have taken, and by wicked hands have crucified and slain: whom God hath raised up, having loosed the pains of death: because it was not possible that he should be holden of it…. Because thou wilt not leave my soul in hell, neither wilt thou suffer thine Holy One to see corruption.

—Acts 2:22–24, 27

Jesus never sinned. Joseph of Arimathea went to Pilate, asking for the body of Jesus so he could bury it in his tomb. Pilate said, "Is He dead already? They told him, "Yes." Why? *Because Jesus gave up the ghost.* No one took His life from Him—He gave it up in obedience to the Father, and for you and me.

This is why, if you are born again, you don't need to fear death or where you will spend eternity!

CHAPTER 3

Fear Exposed

PEOPLE FEAR DEATH! THEY fear even the thought of death, even the subject of death. Sometimes that fear will take different forms. In other words, they say, "I fear flying," but they don't really fear flying; they fear dying. Some are afraid of swimming and water (aquaphobia); some are afraid of heights (acrophobia); some are afraid of being in the house alone (autophobia). People fear all kinds of things. All these fears are rooted in the fear of death. Whatever the fear is, it comes from the fear of death, and makes us subject to bondage, imprisoning us so we cannot enjoy life.

If I can get the fear of death removed from you, you could enjoy life on a level that you haven't enjoyed it before. You'd probably go out and buy yourself a motorcycle and hit the road.

Death is not from God. Death is not a friend of God—it is an enemy of God. Death didn't come from God. He never intended for you to die, and He never intended for you to fear death. If you fear death, it's because you are ignorant about it. I'm coming after that ignorance, and I'm going to torpedo that thing right out of your life so you'll never fear death again.

There Is No Such Thing as an Accident

There's no such thing as accidents—that's a human concept. Things don't just happen. There's cause and effect for everything. The enemy tries to hide why something happened and let you call it an accident.

Somebody wants to give you a free cruise trip. "Well, I don't know about that water. I mean, I'll be out on that water. Something might happen to the boat, and you know, hurricanes come out of nowhere." You respond that way because of fear. A lot of times I did that when I had to go down a certain block. I'd walk a certain way because of the gangs there. It was nothing but fear!

I fly airplanes. You get up to thirty thousand feet and lock in autopilot; it's designed to keep you at thirty thousand feet. Even with turbulence, even with bad weather, it'll keep you at thirty thousand feet. If you grab the controls, pull back, go up a thousand feet, and let the controls go, what will happen? It'll bring you right back down.

Your Subconscious Is Your Autopilot

Your subconscious is your autopilot. It is designed to bring you in line with what you believe. If you believe you're going to be broke every month by the thirtieth, your subconscious will make a way for that to happen without you voluntarily doing anything—and it will never fail! That's how strong a subconscious is. Put a person on a stage to speak to a large audience, and you've just crossed out of their comfort zone. Their subconscious is busy trying to shut that thing down. Some people get hives. Some people have heart palpitations. That's evidence that their bodily functions are trying to keep them from stepping into this new reality and across that comfort line.

Your subconscious is designed to keep you comfortable. That's why people who get divorced may often get divorced again, because divorce was written in their comfort zone. They go into another relationship, and it ends up just like the last one.

Don't Believe the Lie

Many of us have allowed the fear of death to run over us—but it's a lie! Some say that God is the One that caused a person's death prematurely or that He sent a tornado or made somebody sick. These lies are exactly what the devil wants us to believe. Giving in to fear is one of the ways the devil gets in. Fear opens the door to satan like faith opens the door to God.

If you don't know how to combat fear or pray for the situation causing the fear, pray in the Holy Ghost. He's your Intercessor. If you don't know what you should pray for, the Holy Ghost on the inside of you will pray through your spirit in a heavenly language that the devil doesn't understand! Doing this will strengthen you and build up your faith.

Saints, I'm saying this because we've got to stop the fear. The enemy has controlled people, even people in the Church, through fear. The devil controls people's health, relationships, finances, and jobs. Some folks are at jobs they can't stand, but they go to work every day out of fear of losing their jobs and not being able to get other ones. It's bondage, and we've got to step away from that. Now, I'm not saying you should quit your job. You've got to get rid of fear, get strong in your faith, and hear from God.

No More Fear

We've got to get into a place where there is no more fear. Say: **"No more fear!"** Jesus didn't fear death, and He taught His disciples not to fear. Do you remember how Peter feared when Jesus was being condemned and they recognized Peter as having been with Jesus? They said, "Weren't you with Him?" Peter said, "No, I wasn't with Him. I don't even know the man." Peter was fearing for his life then, but what happened later when he got filled with the Holy Ghost? Peter's whole nature changed and he didn't fear any man.

In our evangelism ministry, two women on the team went out to witness and came upon this gentle-man. They said, "Excuse me, we'd just like to share with you to see if you'd like to be saved. Do you know Jesus as your Lord and Savior?"

The man said, "Do you know who I am?"

They said, "No, who are you?"

"I'm chief of this gang. You see those guys across the street in that Mercedes? They're watching my back."

A Gang Leader Gets Saved

The ladies asked, "Well, how about peace? You need peace."

He replied, "How'd you know I needed peace? I move around from hotel to hotel. I have to stay on the go. How'd you know I needed peace?"

One lady said, "Listen, shake my hand. Just touch my hand," and he put his hand in her hand, and fell out under the power of the Holy Ghost. Boom! He hit the sidewalk, and cars pulled up from everywhere, guys jumping out.

"What'd you do to him?" He was lying on the sidewalk.

They said, "Nothing. The Holy Ghost arrested him."

He finally came to himself, got up, and said, "What'd you do to me?"

"Nothing," was their answer again.

He said, "Let me see your hand. Let me see what's in your hand." He saw there was nothing in her hand—and received Christ as his Lord and Savior!

It's Time to Overcome Fear

Think about it. What keeps us from witnessing to somebody? Fear. Fear of how they're going to receive us. You know, all of it's rooted in the fear of death. *What's going to happen to me?* We need to get rid of that fear. Start tomorrow. Step across that line and say, "Devil, anybody that looks mean—he's the one I'm going to witness to." Say: **"No fear here!"**

Now, let's look at 2 Timothy 1:7. It says, "For God hath not given us the spirit of fear; but of power, and of love, and of a sound mind." *Repeat this seven times a day out loud for seven days.*

It's time to overcome fear. Say it: **"I have victory over death and fear."**

CHAPTER 4

God's Wisdom

Proverbs 9:10 says, "The fear of the Lord is the beginning of wisdom." Let's look at a parable Jesus told, a story of two men who had very different outcomes to their lives. We read this in Luke 16:

> There was a certain rich man, which was clothed in purple and fine linen, and fared sumptuously every day: and there was a certain beggar named Lazarus, which was laid at his gate, full of sores, and desiring to be fed with the crumbs which fell from the rich man's table: moreover the dogs came and licked his sores. And it came to pass, that the beggar died, and was carried by the angels into Abraham's bosom: the rich man also died, and was buried; and in hell he lift up his eyes, being in torments, and seeth Abraham afar off, and Lazarus in

his bosom. And he cried and said, Father Abraham, have mercy on me, and send Lazarus, that he may dip the tip of his finger in water, and cool my tongue; for I am tormented in this flame. But Abraham said, Son, remember that thou in thy lifetime receivedst thy good things, and likewise Lazarus evil things: but now he is comforted, and thou art tormented.

—Luke 16:19–25

Here's the situation: two men—one of them was a beggar with sores on his body (but thank God he was saved), and one was rich but didn't know God. The Bible says that when the beggar died, he went into Abraham's bosom.

Sheol, a Holding Place for the Righteous Dead

Before Jesus was crucified and ascended into heaven, the righteous who died went into a holding place called Sheol, an upper region in Hades. Nobody could go to heaven until the blood of Jesus actually paid the price and opened the way, but prior to that, those who believed in His coming were called into Abraham's bosom.

Lazarus died and "was carried by the angels into Abraham's bosom." The rich man died and went to hell. (That doesn't mean that because you're rich, you're going to hell.) But if you're rich (or poor) and not saved, then you're going to hell. See, sometimes rich people think there is nothing else they need because money has become their god, and that's where their trust is.

Note that this passage says he was buried, but in hell he lifted up his eyes. His body was buried, so when you die physically, you separate. Your spirit and your soul stay together, and your body is separated from the real you.

Three Deaths

Jesus preached about hell. There is a hell to shun, and you don't want to go there. I'm going to show you that there are three deaths: physical death, spiritual death, and the second death.

Let's continue: The rich man cried out. He recognized Abraham, so without his body, he was crying.

That means he must have vocal cords, a mouth, and probably some tears. *This is without a body!*

He cried and said, "Father Abraham!" He had recognition, so that means *he had his mind.* "Send Lazarus, that he may dip the tip of his finger in water and cool my tongue; because I'm tormented in this flame." This tells me you can be tormented and in pain *without* your physical body.

Recognizing that there was some water, he said, "Send Lazarus." Even without his body, he was still ordering folks around! If you had a bossy disposition while you lived on the earth, when you die and go to hell, you're still going to have the same bossy disposition down there.

Without a Body You've Still Got Parts

Note that it says, "that he may dip the tip of his finger." Without a body, you've got a fingertip. And the man asked that Lazarus might dip the tip of his finger "in water, and cool my tongue." Without a body, you've got a tongue. This means your body is only a physical representation of everything you've got in the spirit!

The jacket I'm wearing fits me because it is my covering! It is a representation on the outside of what's inside. I can pull it off, and it loses its shape, but I'm still here! My body is going back to the dust, but I'm going to live forever! I know Jesus! God is my Father, and I'll be with Him forever!

You've Got the Mind of Christ

> **Let this mind be in you, which was also in**
> **Christ Jesus: who, being in the form of God,**
> **thought it not robbery to be equal with**
> **God: but made himself of no reputation,**
> **and took upon him the form of a servant,**
> **and was made in the likeness of men:**
> **and being found in fashion as a man, he**
> **humbled himself, and became obedient**
> **unto death, even the death of the cross.**
>
> —Philippians 2:5–8

Here we see Jesus moving in His life all the way to Calvary because this is why He came. He was moving to Calvary, and He was being obedient all the way, but now He got to a place called the Garden of Gethsemane. This was a testing ground. Adam blew it in a garden. Now Jesus was in a garden where He was being tempted to not go to the cross—not because He feared the death of His physical body, but because He didn't want to be separated from the Father, and He knew that was going to happen too.

Jesus prayed, saying, "O my Father, if it be possible, let this cup pass from me: nevertheless not as I will, but as thou wilt" (Matthew 26:39). In other words, He asked that if there was any way that He didn't have to go this route, would God please open it up, but then He said, "Not My will, but Thy will be done!"

Jesus Goes to the Cross for You and Me

Jesus went to the cross for you and me. He was up there, nailed to the cross, and there were two criminals also being executed, one on either side of Him. One was repentant and recognized that Jesus was the Messiah: "And he said unto Jesus, Lord, remember me when thou comest into thy kingdom. And Jesus said unto him, Verily I say unto thee, today shalt thou be with me in paradise" (Luke 23:42–43).

In the Greek, a better translation would be: "I say unto you today, I will meet you in Paradise." Now, what is Paradise? Paradise is where the departed saints who believed in His coming went when they died. It was a holding place called Sheol, or Paradise. It was not heaven but a staging area for all those who were to go to heaven after the spotless blood of Jesus would be shed and pay the price for their sins.

Jesus Goes to Hell for You and Me

Jesus went to hell, suffering the pangs of death. In hell, He was tormented by demons for you and me. While His body was in the grave in that tomb, Jesus was in hell. Your penalty was eternal death, but Jesus took His faith and compressed eternity down to three days.

The Father saw that justice had been satisfied. When He saw Jesus on the cross, He saw you! When He saw Jesus in the grave, He saw you! When He saw Jesus in hell, He saw you! After Jesus had paid the punishment, the Father said, "Get Him up," and Jesus rose from the dead!

"And having spoiled principalities and powers, he made a shew of them openly, triumphing over them in it" (Colossians 2:15). *The Amplified Bible* says it this way: "When He had disarmed the rulers and authorities [those supernatural forces of evil operating against us], He made a public example of them [exhibiting them as captives in His triumphal procession], having triumphed over them through the cross." This means that Jesus has taken back everything satan took from Adam—*everything* he took from humanity!

Jesus returned to that tomb and slipped on that body. Some women came to the tomb and found it empty. As Mary stood weeping outside, Jesus appeared to her. She tried to touch Him, but He said, "Don't touch Me yet! I have not ascended to My Father and your Father." (See John 20:17.)

Jesus Emptied Paradise

Then Jesus ascended to heaven, taking the blood as proof because life is in the blood (Leviticus 17:14). He put it on the Mercy Seat, then went to Paradise where Abraham, Isaac, and Jacob, and that thief He'd spoken to on the cross were all waiting for Him. The Bible says that Jesus preached to the spirits that were in prison and then He led captivity captive! He said, "Come on, boys! Let's go up to glory!"

You don't have to fear death any more. Remember, I told you earlier, you can put death on the shelf and wait until you make an appointment with it. The price was paid. "Therefore if any man be in Christ, he is a new creature: old things are passed away; behold, all things are become new" (2 Corinthians 5:17).

What can send a person to hell? The only thing that can send someone to hell is not believing in Jesus. "For God so loved the world, that he gave his only begotten Son, that whosoever believeth in him should not perish, but have everlasting life" (John 3:16).

A Dead Man Raised to Life

In John 11, there is a well-known story about resurrection life. A man was raised from death by Jesus, as a witness of the Father's glory. His name was Lazarus.

> Now a certain man was sick, named
> Lazarus, of Bethany, the town of Mary and
> her sister Martha. (It was that Mary which
> anointed the Lord with ointment, and
> wiped his feet with her hair, whose brother
> Lazarus was sick.) Therefore his sisters sent
> unto him, saying, Lord, behold, he whom
> thou lovest is sick. When Jesus heard that,

> he said, This sickness is not unto death, but
> for the glory of God, that the Son of God
> might be glorified thereby.
>
> —John 11:1–4

Here's where some people pick out this verse and say, "Well, the sickness is not unto death, but for the glory of God," or "God gets glory out of my being sick," or "He is trying to teach me something through this." They have believed that sickness is from God or somehow glorifies Him, but that's not what He is saying here.

> Now Jesus loved Martha, and her sister,
> and Lazarus. When he had heard therefore
> that he was sick, he abode two days still in
> the same place where he was. Then after
> that saith he to his disciples, Let us go into
> Judaea again. His disciples say unto him,
> Master, the Jews of late sought to stone thee;
> and goest thou thither again?
>
> Jesus answered, Are there not twelve hours
> in the day? If any man walk in the day, he
> stumbleth not, because he seeth the light of
> this world. But if a man walk in the night,

he stumbleth, because there is no light in
him. These things said he: and after that
he saith unto them, Our friend Lazarus
sleepeth; but I go, that I may awake him out
of sleep.

Then said his disciples, Lord, if he sleep,
he shall do well. Howbeit Jesus spake of his
death: but they thought that he had spoken
of taking of rest in sleep.

Then said Jesus unto them plainly, Lazarus
is dead.

—John 11:5–14

Note that this is not what it says in the original
Greek. It says, "Lazarus dies." It doesn't say, "Lazarus
is dead."

And I am glad for your sakes that I was
not there, to the intent ye may believe;
nevertheless let us go unto him. Then said
Thomas, which is called Didymus, unto
his fellowdisciples, Let us also go, that we
may die with him. Then when Jesus came,
he found that he had lain in the grave four
days already. Now Bethany was nigh unto

Jerusalem, about fifteen furlongs off: and many of the Jews came to Martha and Mary, to comfort them concerning their brother. Then Martha, as soon as she heard that Jesus was coming, went and met him: but Mary sat still in the house. Then said Martha unto Jesus, Lord, if thou hadst been here, my brother had not died. But I know, that even now, whatsoever thou wilt ask of God, God will give it thee.

Jesus saith unto her, Thy brother shall rise again.

Martha saith unto him, I know that he shall rise again in the resurrection at the last day.

Jesus said unto her, I am the resurrection, and the life: he that believeth in me, though he were dead, yet shall he live.

—John 11:15–25

If You Believe in Me, You'll Never Die

Notice what Jesus was really saying here: "If you believe in Me, you'll never die." Now, is that talking about physically or spiritually dying? Spiritually. He was saying that if you believe in Him, you'll never die. He was saying that you've done all the spiritual dying you're ever going to do.

When you leave this body, you just step out of it. When anything happens to this body or you decide to leave it, you step out of it. The body just goes limp, and you are gone. The first thing you would probably notice is freedom. Then you'd probably notice that you can comprehend everything now.

In the biblical account, Lazarus died, but Jesus raised him up and Lazarus came alive again. My point is this: If it were God that was the author of death and the destroyer of Lazarus, why would Jesus raise him up? Jesus raised him up because *God didn't have anything to do with that death*. That death was caused by the devil. The devil was trying to kill Lazarus because he was taking care of Jesus. Lazarus was a witness to who Jesus really is—the Messiah!

The Fear of the Lord Is the Beginning of Wisdom

I started this chapter with Proverbs 9:10, which tells us, "The fear of the LORD is the beginning of wisdom." This doesn't mean we should be terrified of God but rather that we should have reverent awe for God, a respect for His power and sovereignty that causes us to want to obey His commandments.

God is the Giver of Life, and He loves you and me. No longer will we fear death! We will attack every place the enemy has come in because God has given us authority through Jesus' Name to do something about it. Say: **"I'm redeemed."**

If you can't say that, and you're ready to receive freedom through believing in Christ, turn to the Conclusion at the end of this book where I show you my path to freedom and blessing. God is no respecter of persons, and He will do the same for you that He has for me.

· CHAPTER 5 ·

God's Promise

I T'S NO ACCIDENT THAT you were born or that you are living on earth at this particular time in history. God has a specific plan and purpose for your life. "To every thing there is a season, and a time to every purpose under the heaven" (Ecclesiastes 3:1).

Now, that's profound by itself. Every one of us has a reason for being here now. Every one of us has a purpose. Your purpose is different from mine. You can tell that by looking at my fingerprints. They are not like yours and not like anybody's all the way back to Adam. I'm unique—and so are you!

God has placed you here for a purpose and a time. One of the worst situations anyone can experience is to go through life without knowing their purpose, without knowing why they're here.

Somebody said that the richest places in the earth are not the oil fields of Kuwait or the diamond and gold mines of South Africa but the graveyards. Why? Because that's where all the potential is buried. Too many people have gone to the grave without ever having known their purpose.

God's Purpose Is for You to Meet the Needs of Others

I think that purpose has a lot to do with your being able to meet the needs of other people. As long as you are fulfilling God's purpose for your life, you can be sure you are protected. God is not going to allow satan to take you out while He is using you to bless others. Let's read Ecclesiastes 3:2: "a time to be born, and a time to die."

Death is inevitable. That means if Jesus tarries, you're going to die. I want to make that plain because I'm about to say some things here that you're going to have to really grasp tightly. They are revelation truths.

Death is considered a very morbid subject that people don't want to discuss. They feel like victims, powerless in the face of death. When death comes in, it's your time: "Whatever will be, will be."

We think that if we are on an airplane or in a car or on a hunting trip (or whatever the situation is), and something happens to us and we die, people will say, "Well, I guess it was just his time." No, my friends. I want to show you that death is inevitable, yes, but you have something to say about when that time comes.

"And as it is appointed unto men once to die, but after this the judgment" (Hebrews 9:27). People take this to mean God has an appointed time to die, but that's not what this verse says. Let's look at a well-known account in the Bible in which Jesus raised a young girl from the dead.

Raised from the Dead

Though everyone thought it was this young girl's time to die, Jesus had compassion on her grieving parents and raised her up. Let's pick up the story here:

> **And, behold, there cometh one of the rulers**
> **of the synagogue, Jairus by name; and when**
> **he saw him, he fell at his feet, and besought**
> **him greatly, saying, My little daughter lieth**

**at the point of death: I pray thee, come
and lay thy hands on her, that she may be
healed; and she shall live. And Jesus went
with him; and much people followed him,
and thronged him.**

—Mark 5:22–24

Jesus was walking with Jairus to his house and a
woman who had an issue of blood stopped Him. She
touched the hem of His garment, virtue flowed into
her, and it drove that infirmity out of her body. She fell
down and told Him *all* the truth. She testified. This
woman had Jesus occupied for a quite a while so that
by the time He was done with her, runners from Jairus'
house came.

**While he yet spake, there came from the
ruler of the synagogue's house certain
which said, Thy daughter is dead: why
troublest thou the Master any further?
As soon as Jesus heard the word that was
spoken, he saith unto the ruler of the
synagogue, Be not afraid, only believe.
And he suffered no man to follow him,
save Peter, and James, and John the brother
of James. And he cometh to the house of**

> **the ruler of the synagogue, and seeth the**
> **tumult, and them that wept and wailed**
> **greatly.**
>
> —Mark 5:35–38

People Haven't Been Taught the Truth about Death

So now Jesus went to the house, and people were weeping and wailing. This is like what you would encounter at a funeral today: "The Lord gave, and the Lord has taken away. Blessed be the Name of the Lord." They are saying this because they're ignorant of Scripture and haven't been taught. Just like the mourners in Jairus' house, people credit death to God. People fear death because they feel they have no control over it. Watch what happened next:

> **And when he was come in, he saith unto**
> **them, Why make ye this ado, and weep? the**
> **damsel is not dead, but sleepeth. And they**
> **laughed him to scorn. But when he had**
> **put them all out, he taketh the father and**
> **the mother of the damsel, and them that**
> **were with him, and entereth in where the**

damsel was lying. And he took the damsel
by the hand, and said unto her, Talitha
cumi; which is, being interpreted, Damsel,
I say unto thee, arise. And straightway
the damsel arose, and walked; for she was
of the age of twelve years. And they were
astonished with a great astonishment.
And he charged them straitly that no man
should know it; and commanded that
something should be given her to eat.

—Mark 5:39–43

Death Isn't from God

Jairus' daughter died, and Jesus raised her back up,
showing that her death wasn't from God. If it had been,
Jesus could not have violated His Father's will. Death is
not a friend. Death is an enemy, and this death didn't
come from God. So now, let's read our opening verse
again in its full context and see what it says.

And as it is *appointed* unto men once to die,
but after this the judgment: so Christ was
once offered to bear the sins of many; and

unto them that look for him shall he appear
the second time without sin unto salvation.
—Hebrews 9:27–28 emphasis added

Appointed refers to an appointment. There is an appointment that you can make with death. In this book, I'm going to show you how to put death in storage until you get ready for it.

Because he has set his love upon Me,
therefore I will deliver him; I will set him
on high, because he has known My name.
He shall call upon Me, and I will answer
him; I *will be* with him in trouble, and I will
deliver him and honor him. With long life I
will satisfy him and show him My salvation.
—Psalm 91:14–16 NKJV emphasis added

What is considered "long life"? The Bible tells us exactly how many years we're supposed to live, but people have missed it because they think our life expectancy is found in Psalm 90:

For all our days are passed away in thy
wrath: we spend our years as a tale that is
told. The days of our years are *threescore*
***years and ten*; and if by reason of strength**

> **they be** *fourscore years*, **yet is their strength**
> **labour and sorrow; for it is soon cut off,**
> **and we fly away.**
> —Psalm 90:9–10 emphasis added

Folks, how many years are threescore and ten? Seventy. And fourscore? Eighty. If you're going by these verses, you will think that the number of years allotted to you to live is seventy years, possibly eighty—if you're good and haven't drunk too much corn liquor.

If you take this and put it in your subconscious, what will your subconscious start doing when you get close to those ages? It'll start shutting down and breaking your system down. You'll start developing symptoms of arthritis, cataracts, and other aging diseases.

People think they've got to be sick to die, so sickness and pain begin to set in because that's what they're believing for. What we believe is going to start manifesting in our life.

God Sets the Number of Man's Years at 120

Seventy or eighty years were given to the Israelites in the wilderness because they disobeyed the Lord. That number wasn't meant for us today. Genesis 6 says, "And the LORD said, My spirit shall not always strive with man, for that he also is flesh: yet his days shall be an hundred and twenty years" (Genesis 6:3). Put 120 years in your subconscious, and all of a sudden, at seventy, you're going to run a marathon! Praise God!

And don't look around at other folks because the whole world is deceived. Don't go by what they think or say. What do they have to do with you? You look at the Bible. Look at Jesus! He's the Author and Finisher of your faith.

The Old Testament Saints Lived Far Longer

Let's look at the life of Abraham. How long did he live on the earth?

> **And these are the days of the years of Abraham's life which he lived, *an hundred threescore and fifteen years*. Then Abraham gave up the ghost, and died in a good old age, an old man, and full of years; and was gathered to his people.**
>
> —Genesis 25:7–8 emphasis added

What does it say? "Then Abraham gave up the ghost." It doesn't say God killed him; it doesn't say anything about Abraham being sick and dying of senility. It just says he gave up the ghost, and died in what? A "good old age, an old man, and full of years."

If we want some examples of long life, why don't we look at Abraham? That's whose faith we follow. I'm changing the picture inside of you. I'm rooting out unbelief and the lies you've been told about life and death. Now, let's go to another man—one of many in the Old Testament who lived a long time on the earth.

> **And Jacob came unto Isaac his father unto Mamre, unto the city of Arbah, which is Hebron, where Abraham and Isaac sojourned. And the days of Isaac were an *hundred and fourscore* years. And Isaac gave up the ghost, and died, and was gathered unto his people, being old and full of days: and his sons Esau and Jacob buried him.**
>
> —Genesis 35:27–29 emphasis added

The days of Isaac were how many? A hundred and fourscore years—that's 180 years. How about Isaac's son, Jacob? "And when Jacob had made an end of commanding his sons, he gathered up his feet into the bed, and yielded up the ghost, and was gathered unto his people" (Genesis 49:33). Now does that sound like somebody sneaked into his room one night and killed him? Get that out of your head.

Here's another great example of long life: "And Moses was an *hundred and twenty* years old when he died: his eye was not dim, nor his natural force abated" (Deuteronomy 34:7 emphasis added). Moses, at 120 years old, still had the eyesight and strength of a young man and he was in good shape!

I pray for you: **"Father, I pray that You will reveal Your promise of long life to my brother or sister in the Lord, that they can have a long, satisfying life of 120 years on this earth, should Jesus tarry. I rebuke every sickness, every lie, and unbelief that has held my friend in bondage to the traditions of man. I declare today you are free, in Jesus' Name!"**

Redemption Revealed

> **Then cometh the end, when he shall have**
> **delivered up the kingdom to God, even**
> **the Father; when he shall have put down**
> **all rule and all authority and power. For**
> **he must reign, till he hath put all enemies**
> **under his feet. The last enemy that shall be**
> **destroyed is death.**
>
> —1 Corinthians 15:24–26

"FOR HE MUST REIGN, till he hath put all enemies under his feet." Who is Paul talking about here? Jesus! Jesus must reign until *all* enemies are put under His feet—and the last enemy to be destroyed is death.

How will death be destroyed? Hebrews 2:14 tells us this: "Forasmuch then as the children are partakers of flesh and blood, he also himself likewise took part of the same; that through death he might destroy him that had the power of death, that is, the devil."

Here the word *destroy* looks like *annihilate*. However, that's not correct. You cannot annihilate a spirit. If something is a spirit, it cannot be annihilated or destroyed, meaning brought to nothing.

The body can be destroyed because the body is a carcass, and if you leave it on the ground long enough, it'll go back to the dust. However, a spirit will live on somewhere.

The Devil Has the Power of Death

The Scripture tells us who had the power of death. The devil had the power of death. How did the devil get this power? "Sin came into the world through one man, and his sin brought death with it. As a result, death has spread to the whole human race because everyone has sinned" (Romans 5:12 GNT).

"Well, I didn't do nothing too bad," you might say. It's not what you did; it's how you were born. You were born in sin. That's why the apostle Paul said, "Even when I try to do right, I'm doing wrong." (See Romans 7:18–19.) What was he saying? He was saying that inside of me I have the nature of the devil. Even when I try to do right, the devil puts some pressure on me, and I end up doing wrong again.

Then Paul said, "Who's going to save me from this? Thanks be to God" (See Romans 7:24–25). Why? Jesus changed the nature. If He didn't change your nature, you'd still be a pig.

Here's my pig story: A man had a pig that he cleaned up. He put the pig in the bathtub, shampooed him, and put some cologne and a bowtie on him. Then the man had to go to the store, but he left the back door open, and the next thing you know, he came back, and the pig wasn't in the house. He looked out back, and the pig was back in the mud. Why? Because that's its nature. You can wash a pig up and put some sweet-smelling sauce on him, but he is still a pig.

Don't Marry an Unbeliever

This is why a saved person cannot marry an unsaved person. If you're married to one already, that's when we pray to get them converted. However, if you're not married, you're not even supposed to even date an unbeliever. The Bible says that evil communication will corrupt good manners. The first thing you ought to ask a person is, "Are you saved?" Don't think just because they quote Scripture that they're saved because the devil knows more Scripture than anybody.

Before I got saved, I used to cry. I used to get sympathy that way. That was my method: "Don't do me like this, baby." It was nothing but a front. See, you can't believe that. Don't be drawn into sympathy.

The devil had the power of death, but look at the part of Hebrews 2:14 that says this: "He also himself likewise took part of the same," meaning flesh and blood. That's Jesus. He became a man—flesh and blood—so that He could take our place of punishment and destroy the works of the devil.

Jesus Has the Keys of Hell and Death

As I mentioned before, you can't destroy a spirit, so in this verse the word *destroy* basically means that Jesus will render the devil *powerless*. Jesus came to destroy the enemy's ability to wield death, and make it of non-effect. Jesus took the power of death away from satan. "*I* am he that liveth, and was dead; and, behold, I am alive for evermore, Amen; and have the keys of hell and of death" (Revelation 1:18).

Keys symbolize authority. Jesus passed that authority to the Church (to the believer), so satan no longer has the power of death over the believer. Now he can no longer wield death over our lives. Hebrews 2:15 says, "And deliver them who through fear of death were all their lifetime subject to bondage."

Jesus Came to Redeem Mankind from Death

Jesus came to repair the breach and redeem mankind. He came to pay for what man did and change mankind's nature back to what God originally intended. How did Jesus come? He came through a virgin, whose name was Mary. The Bible says there's only one Mediator between God and man, and that is the Man Christ Jesus. That's all!

Mary was not a deity. Mary was a person who needed to be saved just like you and me. There is nothing in the Scriptures that says we are to pray to Mary, no matter what some denominations practice. If your denomination doesn't line up with the Bible, your denomination is in error. You have a choice. You can either walk with God and believe His Word, or you can walk with your denomination and believe in error.

You Can See Beyond What the Natural Eye Can See

Adam lost his spiritual eyes when he sinned. He could only see with his natural eyesight. When Jesus came, He came not only to redeem us but also to bring us back to the place in which we could receive revelation knowledge and go beyond the natural!

In John 8, Jesus gave revelation knowledge to the religious leaders of His time, but they only saw with their natural eyes and according to their traditions. Jesus told them, "Ye do the deeds of your father. Then said they to him, We be not born of fornication; we have one Father, even God" (John 8:41).

They claimed that God was their Father, but Jesus disagreed. Watch how He responded:

> **Jesus said unto them, If God were your Father, ye would love me: for I proceeded forth and came from God; neither came I of myself, but he sent me. Why do ye not**

**understand my speech? even because ye
cannot hear my word.**

—John 8:42–43

Note what Jesus was saying: "I came from the Father." Now we know that the Virgin Mary gave birth to Jesus and she had no physical relationship with a man. How did she get a baby with no relationship? It was impossible then. Today we have artificial insemination. There's a sperm bank from which the seed is taken and planted in a woman's womb. The next thing you know, a child is conceived. But that did not happen in Mary's life.

The Divine Seed Came Directly from God

The Seed in Mary's body came directly from God—it came into her womb supernaturally. Get this: It was the Seed of the Word of God. In nine months she gave birth to the Son of the Most High God.

Now understand this: Jesus didn't have natural blood because no blood from the woman gets past the placenta. It doesn't go into the baby's body. Jesus' blood came from God alone. It had to come from God because if it came from a man, Abel could've died for your sins, but he could not. God didn't need corrupted blood; God needed *spotless* blood. This perfect blood is the blood that saved you.

Then Jesus continued His teaching to the Jews:

> **Ye are of your father the devil, and the lusts of your father ye will do. He was a murderer from the beginning, and abode not in the truth, because there is no truth in him. When he speaketh a lie, he speaketh of his own: for he is a liar, and the father of it.**
>
> —John 8:44

Two Fathers

There are two fathers. One is a natural father. Everybody has been born of a natural father, and everyone has a spiritual father. In the spirit you can have only one out of two fathers. Either God is your Father, or satan is your father.

When Adam sinned in the garden, he switched fathers. The One who was his father and put him on this earth was God; but by his own sinful act, Adam chose another father, satan, and became the first man born from life to death. From that point on, everybody was born with Adam's fallen nature so everybody must be born again to become a child of God!

God can't be your Father unless you're born again. Some people have heard this old saying about the fatherhood of man: "God is the Father of everybody." *That's not true.* God is *Creator of all*, but He is Father only to those who have become His children by being born again. "But as many as received him, to them gave he power to become the sons of God, even to them that believe on his name" (John 1:12).

Don't Try to Evaluate Yourself

Know this: you can't be a child of God unless you receive Jesus as your Savior and Lord. Sin has spread to every man so don't try to evaluate whether you are a sinner. Even if you were born in a clean hospital room and raised there for forty years, and never cussed anybody out or told anybody off or lied, you would be in trouble. If you died in that shape, you would bust hell wide open! It's not about how you are acting. It's how you were born. Everybody's got to be born again to enter the Kingdom of God!

"Your father," Jesus said, "is the devil and the lusts of your father ye will do." Stop looking at lust only as some man lusting after a woman. It refers to pressure. It means that because people have a fallen nature, satan can deceive them and put pressure on them to do his will.

Some people don't know who their daddy is, or they think somebody is their daddy and find out forty years later that it's a lie, and they never know who their biological daddy really is. This is sad, but you know who your Daddy is when you get saved. You know exactly who He is—Father God! He won't abandon you or reject you like some earthly fathers. God will love you and be your Daddy forever.

Dominion Restored

As I mentioned in an earlier chapter, the Bible says in 1 Corinthians 15 that Jesus was the last Adam. Jesus came to show you how Adam (before the Fall) took dominion over the earth. Through Jesus, God has called you to have dominion too—in your workplace, community, and nation.

"For as the Father hath life in himself; so hath he given to the Son to have life in himself" (John 5:26). What kind of life is that? That is spiritual life. That is the life of God—eternal life. Jesus brought that life to the earth because you and I need that life so that we can live again.

"God said, Let us make man in our image, after our likeness: and let them have dominion" (Genesis 1:26). God is saying that man is the one to whom He gave authority on earth, but sadly, Adam turned it over to the devil when he sinned. It took Jesus to come and function as a man to restore that dominion to His people, the Body of Christ, the Church.

We Operate in Dominion through Prayer

If God needs to do something in the earth, what needs to happen? He needs you to ask for it. It's called prayer. He needs your permission and participation because you now have the authority on earth.

One of the primary and most important tasks God's trying to accomplish is to get the saints to pray. However, prayer meetings are sometimes not well-attended, and prayer itself is too often the last thing we do. This shouldn't be. This is time when we get to communicate with Almighty God so He can change things in our lives.

There has never been a more urgent time to use your spiritual authority in prayer than now. It is past time to dominate the forces of evil and set the captives free. "How long will ye judge unjustly, and accept the persons of the wicked? Selah. Defend the poor and fatherless: do justice to the afflicted and needy. Deliver the poor and needy: rid them out of the hand of the wicked" (Psalm 82:2–4).

We Have Been Redeemed from Death

We have been redeemed. We have been brought out of darkness into the marvelous light, out of the kingdom of darkness into the Kingdom of God's dear Son. As Kingdom citizens, we operate in The Blessing through our faith.

> **Christ hath redeemed us from the curse of the law, being made a curse for us: for it is written, Cursed is every one that hangeth on a tree: that the blessing of Abraham might come on the Gentiles through Jesus Christ; that we might receive the promise of the Spirit through faith.**
>
> —Galatians 3:13–14

It's going to have to be your faith that gives you the ability to receive this inheritance of The Blessing of Abraham. In the Kingdom, dominion has been restored to us. We are able to live on a higher plane than natural man. We are not limited by the standards of natural man. We apply the standards of the Bible instead, and allow the Holy Ghost to be our Teacher. He's going to show us how to get back to that level on which we were created to live and operate in Kingdom authority.

You have the same life, or anointing, in you that Jesus has. He told His disciples this (and it's still true for us today):

> **I assure you, most solemnly I tell you, if anyone steadfastly believes in Me, he will himself be able to do the things that I do; and he will do even greater things than these, because I go to the Father.**
> —John 14:12 AMPC

What was Jesus doing? He was teaching, preaching, and healing. He was casting out devils and setting people free. He was raising the dead.

Jesus Stopped a Funeral

> **Soon afterward Jesus went to a town named Nain, accompanied by his disciples and a large crowd. Just as he arrived at the gate of the town, a funeral procession was coming**

out. The dead man was the only son of a woman who was a widow, and a large crowd from the town was with her. When the Lord saw her, his heart was filled with pity for her, and he said to her, "Don't cry." Then he walked over and touched the coffin, and the men carrying it stopped. Jesus said, "Young man! Get up, I tell you!" The dead man sat up and began to talk, and Jesus gave him back to his mother.

—Luke 7:11–15 GNT

We Can Live in a Place of Protection

Since we have been redeemed from death, we are also redeemed from harm and danger. "We are sure that God's children do not keep on sinning. God's own Son protects them, and the devil cannot harm them" (1 John 5:18 CEV).

This doesn't mean that we never sin or make a mistake; it just means that we don't make a lifestyle of practicing sin. The King James Version says the wicked one can't even touch you!

Paul Shakes Off a Snake

> Once we were safe on shore, we learned that we were on the island of Malta. The people of the island were very kind to us. It was cold and rainy, so they built a fire on the shore to welcome us. As Paul gathered an armful of sticks and was laying them on the fire, a poisonous snake, driven out by the heat, bit him on the hand. The people of the island saw it hanging from his hand and said to each other, "A murderer, no doubt! Though he escaped the sea, justice will not permit him to live." But Paul shook off the snake into the fire and was unharmed.
>
> —Acts 28:1–5 NLT

Did the snake kill Paul? No! He was in the place of God's protection. Your protection isn't natural; it's supernatural.

Resist the Devil, and He Must Flee

The Bible says, "Submit yourselves, then, to God. Resist the devil, and he will flee from you" (James 4:7 NIV). Submit to the authority of God's Word. Then when you resist the devil, he'll flee from you. The devil's not going to flee if you're living in rebellion or some other sin, or if the world's got your attention more than God.

Resisting the devil is not only important for your own life but for others' lives too. God is sending you out to heal the sick, deliver the oppressed, and raise the dead just like Jesus. You've got to have the Word firmly planted in your heart so that it comes out your mouth when you tell the devil, "Go!" Like the centurion, whose servant Jesus healed, you've got to understand authority. You've got to submit to God's authority before the devil will submit to your authority.

You Can Cast Out Unclean Spirits

The disciples learned a lesson on how to use their authority when Jesus sent them out to minister to the people.

> Jesus called his twelve disciples to him and gave them authority to cast out evil spirits and to heal every kind of sickness and disease.... Jesus sent them out with these instructions: "Don't go to the Gentiles or the Samaritans, but only to the people of Israel—God's lost sheep. Go and announce to them that the Kingdom of Heaven is

near. Heal the sick, raise the dead, cure the lepers, and cast out demons. Give as freely as you have received!"

—Matthew 10:1, 5–8 TLB

You can do the works Jesus and the disciples did. God has an inheritance for you—you've been called to have dominion! It starts when you change your thinking. How do you receive your inheritance? By faith! If you've got a situation in your marriage and you want to fix it, God has a way for you to fix it.

Ask for the Wisdom of God

God has a way for you to fix your marriage, your health, your finances, or any other matter, but it's only found *in the wisdom of God.* How do you receive God's wisdom? Ask for it, and believe you receive wisdom for your situation.

If any of you lack wisdom, let him ask of God, that giveth to all men liberally, and upbraideth not; and it shall be given him. But let him ask in faith, nothing wavering. For he that wavereth is like a wave of the sea driven with the wind and tossed. For let

**not that man think that he shall receive any
thing of the Lord. A double minded man is
unstable in all his ways.**

—James 1:5–8

Understand this: you can ask God for wisdom, but you must ask in faith and set aside all fear and doubt. He will give you the answers you need if you do not waver in your faith. You can't be believing one thing one day and something else the next.

Decree What You Want to See

We've got to make a decree, declaring a thing and watching it come to pass. We are royalty—kings and priests. A king decrees a thing, and he doesn't get down off his throne and start worrying about it afterward. He sits right there and tells you what to do.

You are a king and a priest in the Kingdom of God. You're seated together in heavenly places with Jesus, so start using your authority now! Say, "Devil, let me tell you what to do. I want you to get out of here, and don't come back!" All you've got to do is believe what you say, and he will leave.

You Have Power over the Power of the Enemy

You have dominion and power over all the power of the enemy. Look at the results the disciples experienced when Jesus commissioned them to stomp on satan and his demons.

> **And the seventy returned again with joy,**
> **saying, Lord, even the devils are subject**
> **unto us through thy name. And he said**
> **unto them, I beheld Satan as lightning**
> **fall from heaven. Behold, I give unto you**
> **power to tread on serpents and scorpions,**
> **and over all the power of the enemy: and**
> **nothing shall by any means hurt you.**
>
> —Luke 10:17–19

What's another word for *power*? Authority. Jesus gave His disciples authority over all the power of the enemy—and He gives you that same authority today. Now who has the power? *You do.* Who's backing up your power? *God.* What's going to hurt you? *Nothing.*

Saints, if we get this in our spirits, there's nothing we can't do in the Lord. We need to be combat-ready troops. We need to be people that aren't ashamed of the gospel of Jesus Christ! Let's share the good news with a hurting, dying world. We've been redeemed from death, and they can be too!

Conclusion

FAITH WORKS BEYOND THE grave! Some of you reading this book right now are saved, even though your grandmama's gone to be with the Lord. Before she left here, she said, "Lord, save my grand-baby," and God didn't stop working on answering her prayers even though she's in heaven now. She's gone, but faith is still on the job!

God raised Jesus up bodily. He defeated the devil in open combat, taking back the authority. Jesus said, "I am He who was dead." He said, "Don't make any mistake, I was dead, but I got born again. I'm called the firstborn from the dead of many brethren. Now because I live, you can live" (author's paraphrase, a.k.a. the Winston translation).

He walked back to that tomb, slipped on that body, and was glorified, and now He can walk through a wall and sit down and eat fish with the boys. He's alive! In John 20, when Jesus came out of that tomb, Mary tried to touch Him, but He said, "Touch Me not because now I'm functioning as a High Priest. You see, I've got to go before the throne. I've got to take something called the blood because the blood speaks and it declares better things than that of Abel."

You see, Abel's blood cries out vengeance! An eye for an eye, a tooth for a tooth, but the blood of Jesus cries out, "Mercy." MERCY! MERCY! MERCY! Every time God looks at you, He looks through the blood! The blood cries out, "MERCY!" Every time you do something wrong, plead the blood! The blood cries out on your behalf, and you are forgiven.

If you're not where you should be, it's no accident that you're reading this book. A lot of times we think we discover truth ourselves, my friend, but you can't just stumble upon this much truth because the devil won't allow it. Somebody's been praying for you to get saved or come back home and get right with God.

Know this, I want to give you Good News—there's no situation that you've got that He can't fix. I don't care how badly you've messed up, God can turn it around.

My Story

I thought my life was just fine. Because I'd gone to church when I was a little boy, I thought I was A-OK, but did you know you can be in church but not have the church in you?

So, what happened? I got older, sick in body, head over heels in debt, job performance going down, relationships breaking up, everything going wrong. I cried out one night, "Lord, would You please help me?" The Bible says, "Whosoever shall call upon the name of the Lord shall be saved" (Romans 10:13). Realize now, He won't violate your free will. You want to go to hell? He'll protect your right to go there, but He desires that all be saved.

"God so loved the world that He gave His only begotten Son, that whoever believes in Him should not perish but have everlasting life" (John 3:16 NKJV).

God loves you. I'd like the privilege of praying with you just like they prayed for me that night up on the north side of Chicago. That prayer turned my life around forever. The man of God laid hands on me, and after that, the power of God went through my body, healed me instantly, and then He brought me totally out of debt, raised me to the top of the ladder in sales at IBM, and later gave me a worldwide ministry, television broadcast, and several businesses that I preside over today. I'm telling you what He did for Bill Winston, He's ready to do for you.

If you're ready to receive Jesus as your Savior and Lord, and begin a brand-new life, repeat this prayer or use your own words. God hears your heart.

> *"Dear Lord, I come to You now just as I am. You know my life. You know how I've lived. Forgive me, Lord; I repent of my sins. I believe Jesus Christ is the Son of God and that He died for my sins. I believe that on the third day He was raised from the dead. Lord Jesus, I ask You to come into my heart and live Your life in me and through me. From this day forward, I give my life to You. In the Name of Jesus I pray. Amen."*

Anyone who belongs to Christ is a new person. The past is forgotten, and everything is new.

—2 Corinthians 5:17 CEV

Prayer for the Baptism of the Holy Spirit

My Heavenly Father, I am Your child, for I believe in my heart that Jesus has been raised from the dead and I have confessed Him as my Lord. Jesus said, "How much more shall your heavenly Father give the Holy Spirit to them that ask Him" (Luke 11:13). I ask You now in the Name of Jesus to fill me with the Holy Spirit. I step into the fullness and power that I desire in the Name of Jesus. I confess that I am a Spirit-filled Christian. As I yield my vocal organs, I expect to speak in tongues as the Spirit gives me utterance in the Name of Jesus. Praise the Lord! Amen.

Scripture References

- John 14:16–17
- Luke 11:13
- Acts 1:8
- Acts 2:4
- Acts 2:32–33, 38–39
- Acts 8:12–17
- Acts 10:44–46
- Acts 19:2, 5–6
- 1 Corinthians 14:2–15
- 1 Corinthians 14:18, 27
- Ephesians 6:18
- Jude 20

William (Bill)
Samuel Winston

B ILL WINSTON IS THE visionary founder and senior pastor of **Living Word Christian Center** in Forest Park, Illinois.

He is also founder and president of **Bill Winston Ministries**, a partnership-based global outreach ministry that shares the gospel through television, radio, and the internet; the nationally accredited **Joseph Business School** which has partnership locations on five continents and an online program; the **Living Word School of Ministry and Missions**; and **Faith Ministries Alliance (FMA)**, an organization of more than 800 churches and ministries under his spiritual covering in the United States and other countries.

The ministry owns and operates two shopping malls, **Forest Park Plaza** in Forest Park and **Washington Plaza** in Tuskegee, Alabama.

Bill is married to Veronica and is the father of three, Melody, Allegra, and David, and the grandfather of eight.

Books by Bill Winston

- *Be My Witness: Demonstrating the Spirit, Power, and Love of God*
- *Born Again and Spirit-Filled*
- *Climbing without Compromise*
- *Divine Favor — Gift from God, Expanded Edition*
- *Faith and the Marketplace: Becoming the Person of Influence God Intended You to Be, Revised and Expanded Edition*
- *Faith in the Blessing*
- *Imitate God and Get Results*
- *Possessing Your Mountain*
- *Power of the Tongue*
- *Revelation of Royalty: Rediscovering Your Royal Identity in Christ*
- *Seeding for the Billion Flow*
- *Supernatural Wealth Transfer: Restoring the Earth to Its Rightful Owners*
- *Tapping the Wisdom of God*
- *The God Kind of Faith, Expanded Edition*

- *The Kingdom of God in You: Releasing the Kingdom, Replenishing the Earth, Revised and Updated*
- *The Law of Confession: Revolutionize Your Life and Rewrite Your Future with the Power of Words*
- *The Missing Link of Meditation*
- *The Power of Grace*
- *The Power of the Tithe*
- *The Spirit of Leadership: Leadership Lessons Learned from the Life of Joseph*
- *Training for Reigning: Releasing the Power of Your Potential*
- *Transform Your Thinking, Transform Your Life: Radically Change Your Thoughts, Your World, and Your Destiny*
- *Vengeance of the Lord: The Justice System of God*

Some books are available in other languages.

Connect with Us!

Connect with Bill Winston Ministries on social media.

Visit www.billwinston.org/social to connect with all of our official social media channels.

Bill Winston Ministries

P.O. Box 947

Oak Park, Illinois 60303-0947

(708) 697-5100

(800) 711-9327

www.billwinston.org

Bill Winston Ministries Africa

22 Salisbury Road

Morningside, Durban, KWA Zulu Natal 4001

+27(0)313032541

orders@billwinston.org.za www.billwinston.org.za

Bill Winston Ministries Canada

P.O. Box 2900 Vancouver BC V6B 0L4

(844) 298-2900

www.billwinston.ca

Prayer Call Center

(877) 543-9443